AuthorHouse™
1663 Liberty Drive
Bloomington, IN 47403
www.authorhouse.com
Phone: 1 (800) 839-8640

Because of the dynamic nature of the Internet, any web addresses or links contained in this book may have changed since publication and may no longer be valid. The views expressed in this work are solely those of the author and do not necessarily reflect the views of the publisher, and the publisher hereby disclaims any responsibility for them.

Any people depicted in stock imagery provided by Getty Images are models, and such images are being used for illustrative purposes only.
Certain stock imagery © Getty Images.

This is a work of fiction. All of the characters, names, incidents, organizations, and dialogue in this novel are either the products of the author's imagination or are used fictitiously.

This book is printed on acid-free paper.

ISBN: 978-1-7283-2824-9 (sc)
ISBN: 978-1-7283-2823-2 (e)

Library of Congress Control Number: 2019914563

Print information available on the last page.

Published by AuthorHouse 09/25/2019

authorHOUSE®

WILLIE THE WINNER

By Tawanna Croom

"Willie...Willie... time to wake up dear, breakfast is almost ready and you don't want to be late to Winners Mountain today" said Willie's mother. Her voice was sharp and loud. Willie woke up out of his sleep quickly. Just then he remembered what today was, "Oh, boy! Today is the day I get to go up to Winners Mountain for the big conference." Willie was so excited because this was going to be his first trip to Winners Mountain all by himself. Now that he was finally old enough, his parents trusted that he could go the journey alone. Willie was determined not to let them down. He knew he was able to make it up the mountain that day and he could hardly wait to get there.

So out of bed he leaped, he got dressed and joined the rest of the family at the breakfast table. Willie's dad, Walter was sitting at the head of the table and smiled proudly as Willie said the table blessing.

> *God is good, God is great and we thank you for this food. And God thank you for going with me today to Winners Mountain. I know that I can do all things because of you. Amen*

"Thank you, son. So, are you ready for your big solo trip?"

"Yes, Dad I have my map you gave me and I am confident that I can make this trip all by myself. I just can't wait to see all the winners. I am going to take lots of pictures with all of them!"

As the family finished breakfast, Mrs. Winner handed Willie a small gold bag. "Well son, the time has come for me to give you the family treasure bag of golden nuggets."

"Family treasure bag? I did not know we had such a thing, what is that, Mama?"

"Well, Willie it is something that has been in the family for generations. Your great, great Grandfather, Woodrow Winner, created it and passed it down to his son. Now that your big day is here, it is time for you to take it. But you must not open it – until you are off and on your way. But be careful to only take out one golden nugget at a time. We promise you that whatever you need most and when you most need it – will come to you from the treasure bag of golden nuggets" explained Mrs. Winner.

"Yes, Mama– I promise to use the bag the way you have said. I better get going now if I'm going to make it there on time" Willie said quickly as he made a dash for the door.

"Okay son, we love you and we expect that today will be a great day for you, don't forget to call us when you get there!" yelled Mr. Winner.

So off Willie went as happy as he could be about his days journey. He whistled while he walked. He even sang his favorite songs as loud as he could.

As Willie was entering the forest that led to the wooded trail he noticed one of his school friends in the woods climbing up a huge tree. Willie wanted to know why Stanley Spectator was climbing this tree. "Hey Stanley!" "Oh, hi Willie" "What are you doing? Why are you climbing up that tree? It's not a fruit tree, you know." Said Willie "Oh I know that, I am not looking for anything to eat. I am looking to get a good spot to see..." explained Stanley. "See what?" asked Willie.

"Well, I heard that there's a tree in these woods that will let you see everyone who goes up Winners Mountain and I figure this must be that tree. I want to be sure to see all the people as they head up to the mountain today for the Winners Summit, I like to watch all the happenings."

"Watch! Why are you watching why not just go up the mountain yourself?"

"Oh no way! I could never even dream of going up that mountain myself. It's only for special people. It's not for me. Nobody in my family ever went to the actual mountain. We've always been happy with watching all the people instead. So that's what I am going to do, stay right here and watch. Besides, I bet it's a lot harder to get up that mountain than it looks. So, no thanks! I am not about to wear myself out trying. I am good right here in this tree."

"Ok, suite yourself. But I am going up that mountain to be a part of the Winners conference, that's actually where I am going now."

"Really! You're going up the mountain? By yourself? Willie, I don't think that is a good idea. Why don't you play it safe and climb up here in the tree and watch it with me?"

"No thanks, Stanley. My whole family has been to Winners Mountain and now it's finally my turn to go too. So, see ya later! I gotta go. I don't want to miss any of it."

"Ok, but you better be careful. The journey is long and it's getting dangerous these days to travel all alone."

As Willie walked away from Stanley Spectator he started to think about what his friend said about how dangerous the journey could be. Then he remembered that he had that family treasure bag. His mother told him whenever he needed to he could take out a golden nugget. He opened the bag and took out one golden nugget that read:

"In life, you can make one of two choices: You can choose to watch those who make things happen or you can choose to be the one making things happen"

Willie laughed out loud as he read the nugget because he knew that he and Stanley had chosen to be two different people. He put the nugget in his pocket and he continued on his journey.

After walking for a while, Willie decided to take a drink at the brook just ahead. When he came closer he noticed a girl at the side of the lake. He walked up to her and saw that it was Deborah Doubtful. "Hello, Deb. How are you?" "Oh, hey Willie, I am thinking about going to that Winners conference today but I see on my map that I am not even half way there yet and I am so tired already. I doubt if I can make it all the way."

"Sure you can." Said Willie. The fresh drink of water will refresh you and then you can keep going forward."

"No, I don't think so Willie. My feet hurt, I am hungry and very tired. Besides, I doubt if the Summit is even worth all of this. I am going to turn around and go back home. My parents were right, they doubted I could make it that far. I am going home."

"Ok, suite yourself. But I am getting a drink and then continuing the journey. I believe it's going to be well worth the effort. See you later, Deborah." Willie filled his water bottle and headed for the mountain. After all, it was in his view now he could begin to see its peak.

Just as Willie was walking along, he thought about what Deborah Doubtful said. Not that he doubted himself at all. But he felt that now was a good time to read another golden nugget.

"Whatever you think about yourself you become"

Wow! Willie thought to himself about this golden nugget and he was happy about how he was thinking about himself. He was thinking that he could indeed make the journey. It was not too far for him to travel and that it would be worth the trip. He put the nugget in his pocket and kept moving forward.

Willie was making good progress toward the mountain just when he heard something in the bushes. He went to take a look. It was a friend from his old school. He was surprised to see Fredo Fearful all curled up and shaking terribly. "Fredo?"

"Aaaahh!" Fredo screamed in fear. "You scared me, Willie." I thought that you were one of those mean people who are going to that Winners Mountain today."

"Um, you are part right Fredo, I am going to the Summit today but I am not mean and I don't think the Summit will be full of mean people either. After all, they are winners!" explained Willie.

"Yeah well, my parents told me to stay away from those people because they have lots of money and they are very mean to those who don't. I am not going anywhere near that mountain."

"No, no, Fredo, you are thinking all wrong. The people at the summit are happy people and they like to see others happy. Tell you what, why don't you come with me to the Summit and then you can see for yourself."

"Not me, I have too much fear to even go near the mountain. Besides, I don't think my parents would tell me something that isn't true. You can go if you want to Willie, but I am staying far away."

Willie began walking away from Fredo. He didn't understand why Fredo had so much fear in the first place. Maybe there was a golden nugget that could help him understand this more. He opened the family treasure bag and pulled out another golden nugget:

"F.E.A.R. stands for false evidence appearing real"

Willie thought Fredo was being quite ridiculous. Why would he choose to fear the people rather than get to know them? Just then, he turned around thinking he might quickly share this nugget with Fredo. However, he had already begun running in the opposite direction away from the mountain. So, Willie put it in his pocket with the other golden nuggets.

The closer Willie came to Winners Mountain, the more excited he became about meeting all the other winners. Oh boy! He thought just a few more miles and I will be at the mountain. I can hardly wait. He began imagining himself already at the conference. He saw himself shaking hands, taking pictures and hearing their exciting stories about their journey. Just then he heard some laughter coming from the huge oak tree. As he looked a little closer, he realized that it was a group of boys playing on a tire that was tied to the tree and they were swinging from it.

"Wee…Wee…wee!" they giggled. "Hey Willie" one of them said. "Why don't you come join us? We could use another set of arms to push the swing."

"How do you know my name?" Willie asked.

"You probably don't recognize us, but we go to your school. We are the Distraction brothers. I am Dennis, this is Dre and that's Demetrius. Where are you going on Saturday afternoon, all dressed up?"

"I am going to Winners Mountain for a conference, I am almost there, so I can't talk long. I don't want to be late."

"A conference? Are you serious? On a Saturday? Why don't you skip that and come have some fun and play here with us?"

"Nah, that's okay guys. There will be other days I can play. Today I must get to Winners Mountain. You three have fun, I guess I will see you around." As he walked away Willie did slightly remember seeing the boys at school but never in class. They were always playing around in the halls.

As he continued, he remembered there was one more golden nugget in his bag that he had not read yet. He took it out and it read:

"In order to be a winner in life, you must be willing to do what others are not willing to do"

Willie was very thankful that he had stayed focused on his journey and not allowed anyone to distract him. Because it was at that moment that he saw the sign up ahead that said – **Winners Mountain this way** ⟶

"So cool! I am just about there. I can hear the music, smell the food and see the Winners from here. A few more steps and I will be at the mountain."

Willie made it to the base of the mountain and noticed the line was for an elevator ride up. "You mean, I don't have to walk up the mountain?" asked Willie to the lady at the registration table. "No, dear. You have done all the hard work by just making the journey. Your elevator will arrive shortly and take you straight to the top. Welcome to Winners Mountain!"

The End

Tawanna earned her M.S. in Organizational Leadership from Cairn University in Langhorne, PA. (formerly known as Philadelphia Bible University) and her B.S. in Accounting and Business Administration from Delaware State University (1991). Outside her career as a licensed Insurance Agent, Business Analyst and Defined Benefit Administrator, she has served as Youth Director, Sunday School teacher and Youth advisor for local church organizations. Tawanna began her quest for personal development after being introduced to great authors such as Napoleon Hill, Wallace D. Wattles, Charles F. Haanel, Dr. Bill Winston and Joseph Murphy. She has taught online courses on the Laws of Attraction to adults but her real passion is to teach the Universal Laws to children. Tawanna believes that children today are capable to grasp these profound truths at very young ages to ensure their lifelong success.

Printed in the United States
By Bookmasters